PRENTICE HALL
professional educator's library

# PUTTING PATTERNS TO WORK

## Building Critical Thinking

## About the Series Authors

**Jeanette Phillips** is principal of the Tenaya Middle School in Fresno, California. She has been a middle-school principal for the past 19 years and before that served as a vice-principal and as a teacher in grades K-12. Jeanette was a co-founder of the California League of Middle Schools in 1978 and continues to serve on its board as Program Chair. She was a member of the Executive Council and Board of Directors for the National Middle School Association for six years and served as the association's President in 1990–91. She received the Distinguished Service Award from the National Middle School Association in 1992, the ACSA Outstanding Educator Award and the California League of Middle Schools President's Award in 1992.

**Carl Zon** has been a teacher, counselor, and administrator in elementary, middle, and high schools in the states of Illinois, Wisconsin, and California. He is currently on the staff of the California League of Middle Schools and California League of High Schools. As a consultant, he has assisted schools and districts with interdisciplinary unit design and made presentations on interdisciplinary instruction as state and national conferences. He has also been a contributing author on many CLMS monographs. He is past president of the California League of Middle Schools and a recipient of the CLMS President's Award for Exceptional Service to Middle Level Education in California (1992).

## About the Authors

**Bruce Bishop** began teaching math in 1976. Since 1986, he has been teaching computer science and math at Scott Valley Junior High in northern California. He is a graduate of the California Math Project and was chosen the California League of Middle Schools' Region 2 Educator of the Year in 1991.

**Gail Jenner** has taught 7th grade English and social studies at Scott Valley Junior High for five years. Before that, she taught high school English, history, sports, and art. A 1977 graduate of the Northern California Summer Writing Project, she has worked as a county writing specialist for many years.

**Mike Rainville** has spent the last 18 years teaching junior high science in the Los Angeles District Unified Schools and at Scott Valley Junior High. He has also taught high school biology and physical science.

**Millie Whipple-Smith** began her career by teaching for three years at the lower elementary level. A native of Scott Valley, she has taught social studies, English, and art at Scott Valley Junior High for the past 10 years.

## Acknowledgments

**Cover Design:** Suzanne Schineller

**Cover Photo:** Rick Iwasaki/Tony Stone Images



Printed in the United States of America.
ISBN: 0-13-433853-7
2 3 4 5 6 7 8 9 10 02 01 00 99 98

# TABLE OF CONTENTS

# ABOUT INTERDISCIPLINARY UNITS

Successful instructional practices make strong connections between the instruction and substance of subject area disciplines and the developmental characteristics of adolescents. Interdisciplinary learning experiences are particularly appropriate for demonstrating not only the complexity, richness, and "connectedness" of knowledge but also its usefulness and application in the lives of students. Well-planned interdisciplinary units show the world operating as a whole, lend coherence to concepts otherwise isolated within specific disciplines, and empower students to use disciplines in concert and to compare and contrast them.

*Putting Patterns to Work: Building Critical Thinking* is an interdisciplinary unit that brings together discipline-based and interdisciplinary perspectives. The unit has been designed using a step-by-step model adapted by Carl Zon and Laurie Aboudara-Robertson from the work of H. H. Jacobs (1989) and J. H. Borland (1986) and further adapted by the Center for Professional Development and Resources. These model steps are described below.

## Selecting and Defining an Organizing Center

Unit development begins with the selection of a topic or organizing center such as a theme, subject area(s), event, issue, or problem. The topic needs to generate interdisciplinary exploration and be interesting and relevant to students. James Beane (1993) has defined eleven themes that express the intersection of young adolescent concerns and more global social concerns. The theme of "transitions," for example, intersects with these categories of concerns—*understanding personal changes* and *living in a changing world.* Concepts and generalizations in state and national curriculum frameworks can also assist in unifying disciplines. Current events, including those in students' daily lives, can be particularly engaging for adolescent learners.

Once a topic is chosen, teachers should explore it by using a spoked wheel as a graphic organizer. The wheel, or organizing center, includes a hub for the topic and spokes for each discipline. Teachers use brainstorming (Osborne, 1963) to define discipline-based perspectives on the chosen topic. Brainstormed associations, including concepts, generalizations, materials, and people, are written next to the related disciplinary spoke(s).

## Creating a Scope-and-Sequence of Guiding Questions

The next step entails organizing the brainstormed associations and creating a scope-and-sequence of guiding questions for the unit. Brainstorming can once again be used to formulate a tentative list of questions. Students can be involved in this process.

Each guiding question should be general in nature, somewhat like a chapter heading in a textbook. The set of questions, three to six in number, must transcend disciplinary lines, flow in a logical sequence, be sensitive to time constraints, lead to answers students need to know, and be stated in language students comprehend. Study of each question should occupy about one week.

## Developing Master and Individual Activity Plans

The guiding questions are now used to develop master and individual activity plans that engage students in purposeful inquiry. Bloom's Taxonomy (1956) provides a model of cognition that can guide the design of an array of activities that elicit critical and creative thinking including: knowledge acquisition, comprehension, application, analysis, synthesis, and evaluation. Master activity plans, prepared as an overview for each guiding question, summarize individual activities.

Individual activity plans for each guiding question contain: the overall activity plan or objective; possible student groupings for the activity; Bloom's thinking process(es) highlighted in the activity; procedures for carrying out the activity; products and outcomes from students; resources needed; and an evaluation scheme.

## Designing an Evaluation Scheme

A comprehensive evaluation scheme is at the heart of successful interdisciplinary teaching and learning. Given the effort required to develop these experiences and the significant departure from traditional discipline-based instruction they represent, teachers must define standards meticulously and capture evidence of student growth assiduously.

Engaging activities including projects are necessary but insufficient guarantees that students benefit from interdisciplinary experiences. Effective evaluation strategies start with thoughtfully selected organizing centers, carefully stated guiding questions, and clearly defined standards and performance expectations for each activity. Students can keep journals and portfolios to document their responses to guiding questions. They can also participate in defining evaluation criteria for their products and performances.

Finally, teachers must define the value-added dimension of interdisciplinary learning by answering this critical question: "What knowledge, skills, and habits of mind do we value in students as interdisciplinary learners?" Otherwise stated, teachers must design interdisciplinary experiences that provide evidence to answer these questions: What is it about interdisciplinary learning that students cannot acquire without using this approach? Are interdisciplinary learners more likely to see connections between disciplines spontaneously? Do they draw cross-disciplinary insights more frequently? Do they use their knowledge from one discipline to strengthen their understanding of the concepts in another? Are they better synthesizers or holistic thinkers?

Heidi Hayes Jacobs has stated: "With its promise of unifying knowledge and modes of understanding, interdisciplinary education represents the pinnacle of curriculum development" (Jacobs, 1989). You are invited to the "pinnacle" of curriculum design and offered this model to assist you in meeting the interdisciplinary learning needs of adolescents.

**—Carl Zon**

## BIBLIOGRAPHY FOR INTERDISCIPLINARY TEACHING

Beane, J. A. (1993): A middle school curriculum: From rhetoric to reality; Columbus, OH, National Middle School Association.

Bloom, B. S., ed. (1956): Taxonomy of educational objectives: The classification of educational goals, handbook 1: Cognitive domain; New York, NY, David McKay.

Cohen, M. (November 1978): "Whatever happened to interdisciplinary education?" Educational Leadership.

Jacobs, H. H. (1989): Interdisciplinary curriculum: Design and implementation; Alexandria, VA; Association for Supervision and Curriculum Development.

Jacobs, H. H., & Borland, J. H. (Winter 1986): "The interdisciplinary concept model: Design and implementation," Gifted Child Quarterly.

Osborne, A. F. (1963): Applied Imagination; New York, NY; Charles Scribner and Company.

# ABOUT THIS UNIT

Patterns exist everywhere, in nature and in the things that people create. These patterns are important because once they are identified, people can use them as tools to decipher and organize meanings and to make choices and predictions. *Putting Patterns to Work: Building Critical Thinking* is an introductory unit, designed for the opening weeks of school. However, the theme of patterns can be revisited throughout the school year.

Guiding Question 1 helps students define terms and recognize patterns in their own lives. Students use a variety of art materials to create their own patterns and make journal entries about personal patterns.

Guiding Question 2 helps students recognize patterns in subject areas they are studying in school. In a variety of lessons, many of which can be done simultaneously, students read novels to explore patterns in fiction writing, research the patterns found in the rise and fall of empires of the past, write poems using the limerick form, analyze the styles used in various artistic periods, make journal entries, and create mathematical patterns of their own. In addition, students learn about healthful eating patterns, discover patterns in different areas of science, and work together to discover human settlement patterns and some of their causes.

Guiding Question 3 gives students the opportunity to discover how people use patterns. By studying the pattern of regular elections in the United States, students discover some of the people and groups whose actions and activities are in part affected by these election patterns. Students also work in groups to discover how climate and geography cause people in the United States to create and implement certain patterns of living throughout the different seasons of the year. The unit concludes with two Final Activities that offer opportunities for students to work in groups to create and demonstrate patterns in a variety of mediums. These two Final Activities are optional, and teachers may wish to use only one.

# INTERDISCIPLINARY WHEEL

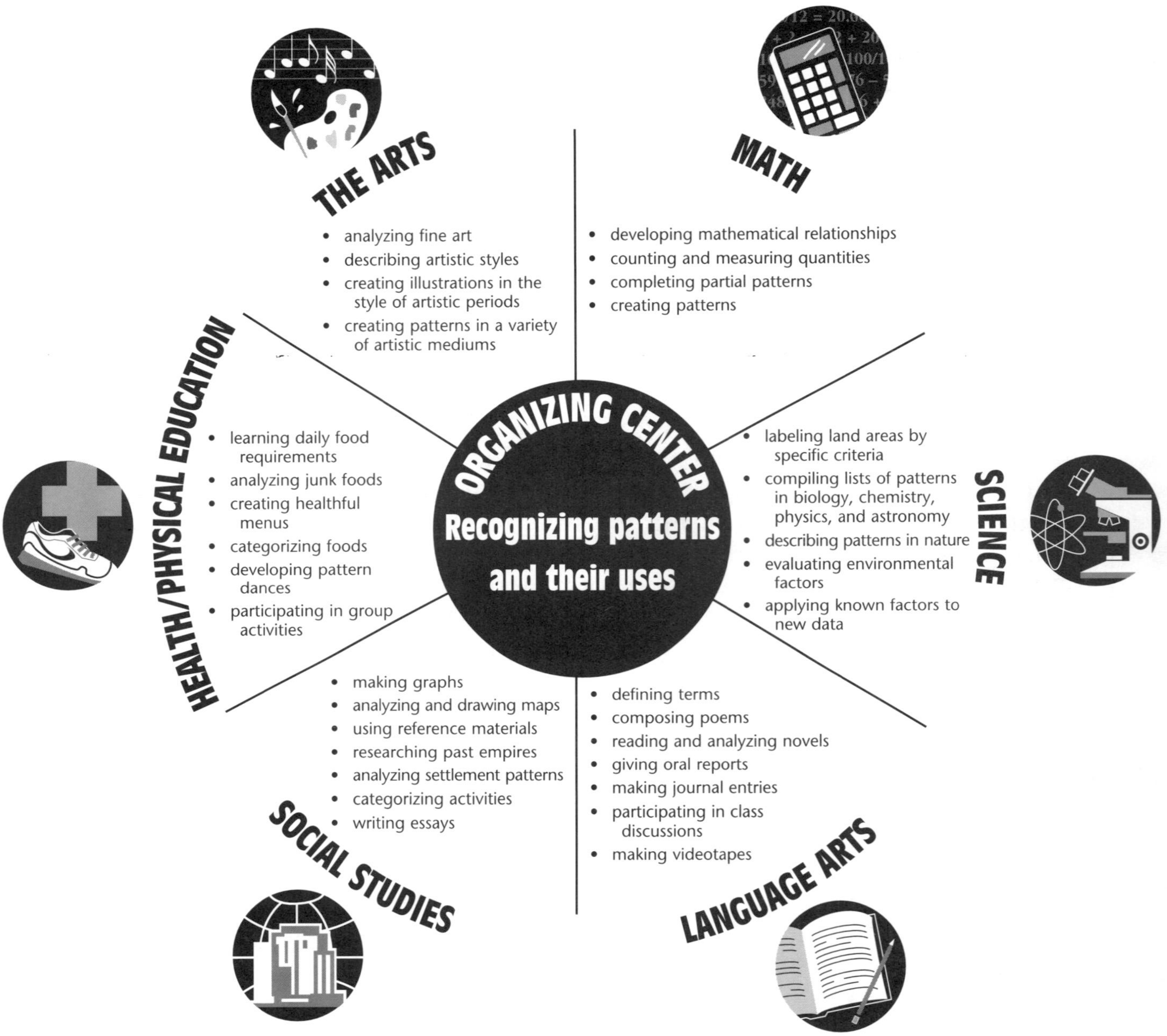


**Source:** Adapted from the work of Heidi Hayes Jacobs, 1988, by Carl Zon, Laurie Aboudara-Robertson, and the California League of Middle Schools.

# GUIDING QUESTIONS

**Organizing Theme:** Recognizing patterns and their uses

**Guiding questions:**

**1.** What are patterns?

**2.** What are some subject area patterns?

**3.** How do people use patterns?

**Source:** Adapted from the work of Heidi Hayes Jacobs, 1988, by Carl Zon, Laurie Aboudara-Robertson and the Redwood Middle School, and the California League of Middle Schools.

# MASTER ACTIVITY PLAN

## Guiding Question 1: What are patterns?

| Activities/Description | Math | Science | Language Arts | Social Studies | Health/Physical Ed. | The Arts | Time |
|---|---|---|---|---|---|---|---|
| **1.1** Defining Terms—defining, describing, and illustrating the concept of a pattern | | ✔ | ✔ | ✔ | ✔ | ✔ | 1 class period |
| **1.2** Looking at Everyday Patterns—recognizing and writing about patterns in everyday life | | | ✔ | ✔ | | | 1 class period |

## 1.1 DEFINING TERMS

### Guiding Question 1: What are patterns?

**Subject Areas:** Science, Language Arts, Social Studies,Health/Physical Education, the Arts

**Grouping:** Whole class, individuals

**Materials:** Art supplies, including paper, colored pencils, colored paper, scissors, and glue;
Thumb tacks;
Illustrations showing patterns

**Bloom's Taxonomy Level:** Knowledge, Comprehension, Inference, Analysis, Application

**Products and Outcomes:** Term definition;
a list of things that include patterns;
art works with patterns

**Time Frame:** 1 class period

---

**Procedure:**

*Pre-class procedure:* Collect the art supplies students will use and make sure enough space is available for displaying student illustrations. Also find and bring to class illustrations of two or three examples of patterns in art and nature. Try to include images of waves in desert sand dunes; tile patterns in flooring; a quilt with a repeat; the three large pyramids at Giza, Egypt; and two or more paintings by Piet Mondrian, such as *Composition with Red, Yellow, and Blue* or *Composition with Yellow and Blue,* or *Composition in Yellow and Black.*

1. Have eight or ten volunteers come to the front of the room and stand in a straight line facing the rest of the class. Then have the volunteers perform "the wave" as is sometimes done by people attending football games and other sporting events. Have the volunteers repeat "the wave" several times and then resume their seats.
2. Write the word *patterns* on the board. Talk with students about "the wave" as an example of a physical pattern that people create. Explain that patterns are the subject of this unit because patterns are something that people encounter throughout life, in school, in daily living, and in society. Knowing about and being able to recognize patterns can help people make good decisions.

MORE

3. Have the class work together to create a definition for the word *pattern* (the arrangement of forms, colors, events, etc., into a model, guide, repetitive design, or example).
4. Show students the illustrations of patterns you have collected. Have the class analyze them and describe what the patterns are and tell why they are patterns.
   - Waves in desert sand dunes: several undulating curves that form on a large body of sand as it is blown by the wind and make a pattern by undulating up and down at roughly the same points
   - Tile patterns in flooring: an intentional arrangement of colors and shapes that form a pattern by being repeated one or more times across the floor
   - A quilt with a repeat: a regularly recurring organization of colors and/or shapes that forms a pattern by utilizing an arrangement that was decided on before sewing began so that all the workers knew ahead of time where to put what parts
   - The Giza pyramids: a distinctive human-made form that was used as a pattern that was then copied to create two additional similar shapes nearby
   - Paintings by Mondrian: an artistic style that uses large, angular blocks of colors and slender black lines to form a style of art that reuses an organization of elements in similar but not identical ways
5. Tell students they are now going to create some patterns of their own. Distribute the art supplies, allowing students to select the colored pencils and/or colored paper as they wish. Have students create their own patterns on two thirds of a sheet of paper and use the remaining space to write out what makes their designs patterns.
6. After students have finished creating their patterns, have them tack their creations to the bulletin board. Then ask volunteers to step to the bulletin board and describe their works to the rest of the class. After several students have spoken, ask the class to study the whole group of works to see if they can recognize any other patterns in the works besides those described. Some of these patterns might involve the materials used, the colors, or the shapes created.

**Evaluation:**

Students should be able to define the term *patterns* and identify some examples.

Students should be able to create a pattern and tell what makes the design a pattern.

## 1.2 LOOKING AT EVERYDAY PATTERNS

### GUIDING QUESTION 1: What are patterns?

**SUBJECT AREAS:** Language Arts, Social Studies
**GROUPING:** Whole class, individuals
**MATERIALS:** Student journals;
Textbooks
**BLOOM'S TAXONOMY LEVEL:** Knowledge, Comprehension, Inference, Analysis
**PRODUCTS AND OUTCOMES:** Journal entry
**TIME FRAME:** 1 class period

---

**Procedure:**

*Pre-class preparation:* The day before this activity, remind students to bring one of their textbooks to class with them tomorrow. Social studies, math, health, or science textbooks would be good choices.

1. Begin by asking students to take out one of their textbooks. Have students look at the table of contents. Help them come to see that their textbooks usually follow a pattern of units, chapters, and lessons with special features interspersed throughout. Then have students turn to the ends of their books to see the index and other support materials such as glossaries and appendixes and, sometimes, answer keys as found in math books. Students should recognize that this pattern of textbook organization can be a useful tool for them in looking ahead to where they will be going in their studies and conceptualizing the "whole" of their course work.
2. Then have students turn back to the tables of contents. Have students select a chapter and turn to it. Ask a volunteer, especially one using a social studies or science textbook, to read the chapter subheads aloud. Then talk with students about how these subheads can be turned into questions that the text itself will answer. Ask the volunteer to again read the chapter subheads aloud. As each subhead is read, ask others in the class to turn the statement into a question and say what will probably be covered in that section of the text. Students should come to see that this process can be an effective study technique that they can regularly employ because their textbooks follow a regular pattern of organization and format.

MORE

3. Ask students to name some of the patterns in school. Answers might include the daily pattern of classes, going from one grade level to the next over a series of years, usually having many more students than teachers in the building, or having well-known start times, lunch times, and dismissal times each day. Have a volunteer write students' suggestions on the board.

   Now ask volunteers to say how people in the class are affected by each of the patterns listed on the board. Help students come to understand that patterns in their lives may be so subtle or well ingrained in their lives that students may not even realize the important role patterns play.

4. Now ask students to think about patterns in their own daily lives, such as their class schedules or their daily routines of when they get up, when they leave for school, and so on. Have volunteers tell the rest of the class about these patterns. Help students come to see similarities and differences between the patterns of various individuals.

5. Have students spend the remainder of the period thinking about their personal patterns and writing about them in their journals. Students should come to understand that different patterns can be equally successful in achieving the same goals.

**Evaluation:**

Students should be able to recognize patterns in the organization of their textbooks and understand that they can use these patterns as a study technique.

Students should be able to recognize some patterns in their own lives and write about these patterns in their journals.

# MASTER ACTIVITY PLAN

## GUIDING QUESTION 2: What are some subject area patterns?

| Activities/Description | Math | Science | Language Arts | Social Studies | Health/Physical Ed. | The Arts | Time |
|---|---|---|---|---|---|---|---|
| **2.1** Finding Patterns in Math–using shapes and sequences to see patterns in math | ✔ | | ✔ | | | | 1 class period |
| **2.2** Discovering Patterns in Science–using science textbooks to discover patterns in science, such as the water cycle | | ✔ | | | | | 1 class period |
| **2.3** Looking at Patterns in Poetry–reading and writing limericks and other poems to see patterns | | | ✔ | | | ✔ | 2 class periods |
| **2.4** Learning about Literature–reading a novel to discover the patterns that the literary form follows | | | ✔ | | | | 2 nonconsecutive class periods |
| **2.5** Tracing the Rise and Fall of Peoples–researching powerful civilizations and empires of the past to discover historical patterns | | | ✔ | ✔ | | ✔ | 3 class periods |
| **2.6** Understanding Why People Live Where They Do–analyzing geography and other factors to understand patterns of human settlement | | | ✔ | ✔ | | | 1 class period |
| **2.7** Finding the "Style" in Art–studying major artistic periods and creating illustrations based on those styles | | | | ✔ | | ✔ | 2 class periods |
| **2.8** Healthful Eating–learning about the Food Pyramid, analyzing the contents of junk foods, creating healthful eating plans | ✔ | ✔ | ✔ | ✔ | | | 1 class period |

## 2.1 FINDING PATTERNS IN MATH

### GUIDING QUESTION 2: What are some subject area patterns?

**SUBJECT AREAS:** Math, Language Arts
**GROUPING:** Whole class, pairs
**MATERIALS:** Patterns in Mathematics activity sheets, 1 per student
**BLOOM'S TAXONOMY LEVEL:** Knowledge, Comprehension, Inference, Analysis, Application, Synthesis
**PRODUCTS AND OUTCOMES:** Completed Patterns in Mathematics activity sheets
**TIME FRAME:** 1 class period

**Procedure:**

1. Begin by having students review together what they have learned about patterns. Discuss the subject of mathematics as having many patterns. Use the multiplication tables as a good example of patterns in mathematics.
2. Tell students that there are many more patterns in mathematics. Divide the class into pairs and distribute the Patterns in Mathematics activity sheet. Tell the student pairs to work together to discover the patterns in each of the items on the activity sheet and to complete the activity sheet. Set a specific time limit for completion of the activity sheet.
3. Walk around the room while the students are working on the activity sheet and provide help as necessary to those student pairs who may be having difficulty.
4. When the time limit is up, have students stop working on their answers, even if everyone is not finished. Go through the items one by one and ask volunteers to explain how they solved each puzzle item and to identify the pattern in each.

*Answers:*

(1) This pattern is the hours of the day in three-hour increments: 5 A.M., 8 A.M., 11 A.M., 2 P.M., 5 P.M., 8 P.M.;

(2) This pattern shows each number multiplied by itself: 2, 4, 16, 256, 65,536;

(3) This is a pattern of prime numbers, meaning they can only be divided by two factors, 1 and themselves: 1, 2, 3, 5, 7, 11, 13, 17, 19, 23, 29;

MORE

(4) This pattern is based on the degrees in a circle, in 45° increments: 0°, 45°, 90°, 135°, 180°, 225°, 270°, 315°, 360°;

(5) This pattern is the last days of each month: Jan 31, Feb 28, March 31, April 30, May 31, June 30, July 31, Aug 31, Sept 30, Oct 31, Nov 30, Dec 31;

(6) This pattern is the sum of the previous two numbers in the sequence: 1, 2, 3, 5, 8, 13, 21, 34, 55, 89;

(7) This pattern of geometric forms has one more side in each succeeding image: 3 sides, 4 sides, 5 sides, 6 sides, 7 sides, 8 sides;

(8) These student-created patterns could include addition or subtraction by the same number, dividing by a same number, etc.

**5.** As a concluding activity, ask students to write on the board and describe for the rest of the class the math patterns they created for their activity sheets. After each volunteer has finished, allow the rest of the class to comment on the pattern, including describing how the pattern would continue past the numbers shown on the board.

After several volunteers have displayed their math patterns on the board, ask the whole class to study the individual patterns to discover if there are any larger math patterns that link one or more of the examples. As students recognize such patterns, ask them to verbally describe the pattern and write the description on the board.

**Evaluation:**

Students should be able to identify, complete, and describe some sample mathematical patterns.

Students should be able to create and describe mathematical patterns of their own.

NAME ______________________ CLASS ____________ DATE ____________

# PATTERNS IN MATHEMATICS

Each of the math puzzles below involves a pattern. Discover the pattern in each by filling in the blanks. Then create a mathematical pattern of your own.

**1.** 5 A.M., 8 A.M., ______, 2 P.M., ______, ______

**2.** 2, 4, ______, 256, ______

**3.** 1, 2, 3, 5, ______, 11, ______, ______, 19, ______, ______

**4.** 0°, ______, 90°, ______, 180°, ______, ______, ______, 360°

**5.** J31, F28, M______, A30, ______31, J______0, J3______, ______31, S30, ______, ______, ______

**6.** 1, 2, 3, 5, 8, ___, 21, 34, ___5, 8___

**7.**  ______ ______ ______

**8.** Use the space below to create a mathematical pattern of your own.

 

# 2.2 DISCOVERING PATTERNS IN SCIENCE

## GUIDING QUESTION 2: What are some subject area patterns?

**SUBJECT AREAS:** Science

**GROUPING:** Whole class, individuals

**MATERIALS:** Science textbooks

**BLOOM'S TAXONOMY LEVEL:** Knowledge, Comprehension, Inference, Analysis, Application, Synthesis

**PRODUCTS AND OUTCOMES:** Lists of things in science that work in or are patterns

**TIME FRAME:** 1 class period

---

### Procedure:

*Pre-class preparation:* The day before the activity, remind students to bring their science textbooks with them to class tomorrow.

1. Begin by asking students to name and describe patterns in science or nature that they may already know about, such as the seasons, tree rings, radio waves, or the shape of a spider web.
2. Ask students to take out their textbooks and use them to make lists of things in science and nature that are or work in patterns. Suggest that students use the table of contents and index for ideas and thumb through the books as well. Set a time limit.
3. At the appropriate time, ask students to read their lists aloud, while two volunteers write the items on the board.
4. When the class list is complete, ask students to organize the items into groups, categorize the groups, and create generalizations about patterns in science such as: minerals have an orderly arrangement of atoms; many things in nature, like many crystals and some plants, grow outward from a central core; or living organisms undergo physical change over time.

### Evaluation:

Students should be able to list and describe some patterns in science.

Students should be able to group individual items into categories that show larger patterns and write generalizations to describe them.

## 2.3 LOOKING AT PATTERNS IN POETRY

### GUIDING QUESTION 2: What are some subject area patterns?

**SUBJECT AREAS:** Language Arts, the Arts

**GROUPING:** Whole class, small groups

**MATERIALS:** Limericks activity sheet, 1 per student;
Art supplies, including a large roll of butcher paper, paints, glue, scissors, and colored paper;
Poetry anthologies

**BLOOM'S TAXONOMY LEVEL:** Knowledge, Comprehension, Analysis, Application, Synthesis, Evaluation

**PRODUCTS AND OUTCOMES:** Completed Limericks activity sheets; group illustrations of selected poems

**TIME FRAME:** 2 class periods

---

**Procedure:**

*Day 1*

1. Divide the class into several groups and allow students to rearrange their desks so that the people in each group are clustered together.
2. Distribute the Limericks activity sheet and tell students that the poetry shown here is in a form called a limerick. Ask students to read each limerick silently and then to work within their groups to discover and list patterns in the limericks. Set a time limit for the student groups to complete their lists.
3. When the time is up, ask a volunteer from each group to tell the rest of the class about the patterns it has discovered. These patterns include:

   - Limericks are humorous.
   - Limericks are five lines long.
   - Limericks are often nonsense poems.
   - The first, second, and fifth lines of a limerick rhyme with each other.
   - The first, second, and fifth lines of a limerick each have three accents, or beats.
   - The third and fourth lines of a limerick also rhyme with each other.
   - The first line often is set up as "There is a/an (person) from (place)."

   Help students come to see that these similarities create a pattern and that the pattern is what defines a limerick.

MORE

4. Have students work in their groups to write their own limericks, using the space available on the bottom of the Limericks activity sheet. Again, set a specific time limit in which the work is to be done.
5. When the work time is over, have the groups take turns reading their limericks aloud to one another. Allow time for the whole class to discuss each limerick and its rhyme scheme and suggest an image that might illustrate the limerick.

*Optional Assignment:* Collect a few examples of haiku, a Japanese form of poetry in three lines of five, seven, and five syllables respectively. Photocopy the haiku and use them in place of or in addition to the limericks.

*Day 2*

*Pre-class preparation:* Check out several books of poetry from the library so that there is at least one book for each of the groups. Be sure one of the books includes Robert Frost's "Stopping by Woods on a Snowy Evening." Mark this poem in the book so you can quickly refer to it later. Also collect the art supplies.

1. Allow students to move their desks around so they are sitting near others in their group. Distribute the books of poetry to each of the groups.
2. Ask students to listen carefully while you read Frost's "Stopping by Woods on a Snowy Evening" aloud to them. Then ask students to suggest images that the poem evokes. Help students come to see that one pattern in poetry is its ability to create strong visual images in the minds of those who read or hear it. Tell students that today they are going to work in groups to create some of these strong images.
3. Ask each group to select a short poem to illustrate. Point out to students the variety of art supplies they have available to create their illustrations; give each group a large sheet of butcher paper to work on. Tell students that part of their work will include an oral presentation (group recitation, individual reading, or acting out, etc.) of their poem to the rest of the class. Give students most of the class period to select and illustrate their poems.
4. When the time limit is up, ask each group to read its poem aloud for the rest of the class. Ask others in the class to describe how each illustration portrays the poem it is created for.

**Evaluation:**

Students should be able to identify the concept of rhyme scheme and how it applies to limericks.

Students should be able to work in groups to write their own limericks, using patterns the class has identified.

Students should be able to recognize the strong visual impact a poem may have and create an appropriate illustration.

NAME ______________________ CLASS ____________ DATE ____________

# LIMERICKS

Read these limericks, and then use the space provided below to write your own.

There was a young farmer of Leeds,
Who swallowed six packets of seeds,
It soon came to pass
He was covered with grass,
And he couldn't sit down for the weeds.

There was a young lady whose bonnet
Came untied when the birds sat upon it.
But she said, "I don't care!
All the birds in the air
Are welcome to sit on my bonnet!"

There was an old man from Peru,
Who dreamed he was eating his shoe.
He awoke in the night
And turned on the light
And found it was perfectly true.

There was an old person of Shields,
Who frequented the valley and fields.
All the mice and the cats,
And the snakes and the rats,
Followed after that person of Shields.

 

# 2.4 LEARNING ABOUT LITERATURE

## GUIDING QUESTION 2: What are some subject area patterns?

**SUBJECT AREAS:** Language Arts

**GROUPING:** Whole class, individuals

**MATERIALS:** Seeing Patterns in Literature activity sheet, 1 per student;
Novels, 1 per student;
Literature textbooks, 1 per student

**BLOOM'S TAXONOMY LEVEL:** Knowledge, Comprehension, Inference, Analysis, Application

**PRODUCTS AND OUTCOMES:** Completed Seeing Patterns in Literature activity sheets

**TIME FRAME:** 2 nonconsecutive class periods

---

**Procedure:**

*Pre-class preparation:* Work with the school librarian to make a list of or set aside a group of novels that are appropriate for the lesson. Also make plans with the librarian for the class to work in the library during most of the first class period of the lesson. Ask the librarian to be available to help students during that class period if at all possible. Also remind students the day before the lesson to be sure to bring their literature textbooks with them to class the next day.

*Day 1*

1. At the start of the period, tell students that this lesson will help them recognize patterns in literature and that they will read a novel and complete an accompanying activity sheet.
2. Distribute the activity sheet, and ask students to take out their literature textbooks. Discuss each of the items on the activity sheet in turn with the whole class. Ask students to find examples of each activity sheet item in their literature textbooks. Talk about how each of the items on the activity sheet is one facet of the pattern that literature frequently follows. Allow students time to ask questions as necessary.
3. Have students collect their belongings and go to the school library. Have the class sit in a group in one section of the library. Distribute the list of books or allow students to select from the group that has been set aside. Suggest to students that they read a page or two of several books before selecting one so they will be best able to find a book they will enjoy reading.

MORE

4. As students select their books, direct them to the checkout desk, and tell them to be sure to note the day when the book is due back at the library.
5. Give students a specific date by which they are to have read their novels and completed the activity sheet. Let students use any remaining class time in this period to begin reading their novels.

*Day 2*

*Pre-class preparation:* Remind students that their completed Seeing Patterns in Literature activity sheets are due the next day and that they should bring the sheets and their novels to class.

1. Begin by asking each student to name the book he or she chose to read. Help students come to see that novels encompass a broad range of topics.
2. Ask volunteers to read each of the activity sheet points aloud. Call on other students to read their responses to each point. Help students come to see the patterns that many novels follow.
3. Have students turn in their completed activity sheets so that you can review and comment on them.
4. Conclude by asking students to discuss other novels they may have read and tell the rest of the class about the settings, characters, plots, narrators, and symbolism in those books.

**Evaluation:**

Students should be able to read novels and recognize that they often follow patterns.

Students should be able to describe the settings, characters, plots, narrators, and symbolism in novels they have read.

NAME ____________________ CLASS __________ DATE __________

# SEEING PATTERNS IN LITERATURE

Read the novel you have selected. As you read, write your answers to these questions. Finish your answers on another sheet of paper if you need more room.

1. The **setting** of a novel is place where the action takes place as well as the historical period in which it occurs. What is the setting of your novel?

______________________________

______________________________

______________________________

2. The **characters** in a novel are the people who carry the story forward. Who are the main characters in your novel?

______________________________

______________________________

______________________________

3. The **plot** of a novel is the series of events that make up the story. A plot has a beginning, a middle, a climax or high point of interest, and an end. What is the plot of your novel?

______________________________

______________________________

______________________________

4. The **narrator** is the person through whose eyes the action of the novel is seen. Many novels are told from the point of view of a single narrator. Sometimes, the narrator knows the thoughts of some or all of the characters. Who is the narrator of your novel and what point of view does he or she have?

______________________________

______________________________

______________________________

5. The **theme** is the central idea of a work. It is the main statement that the author is trying to convey. What is the theme of the novel you read?

______________________________

______________________________

______________________________

## 2.5 TRACING THE RISE AND FALL OF PEOPLES

### Guiding Question 2: What are some subject area patterns?

**Subject Areas:** Language Arts, Social Studies, the Arts

**Grouping:** Whole class, small groups

**Materials:** The Rise and Fall of Peoples activity sheet, 1 per student;
Encyclopedias and other reference books on world history;
Art supplies including colored paper, scissors, glue, paints, colored pencils, and tracing paper;
Student journals

**Bloom's Taxonomy Level:** Knowledge, Comprehension, Inference, Analysis, Application, Synthesis, Evaluation

**Products and Outcomes:** Bulletin board displays;
group presentations to the rest of the class;
completed Rise and Fall of Peoples activity sheets;
journal entry

**Time Frame:** 3 class periods

**Note:** *Plan to leave the group display of Egypt on the bulletin board for use with lesson 2.6. The other displays may be taken down, if necessary, at the end of this lesson.*

---

**Procedure:**

*Pre-class preparation:* Collect encyclopedias and other reference books on world history and place them in one area of the classroom. Divide a classroom bulletin board into five large sections.

*Day 1*

1. Begin by telling students that just as there are patterns in science, math, and literature, there are patterns in the rise and fall of civilizations and empires in history.
2. Divide the class into five groups and assign each group one of the following civilizations or empires to research and report on: ancient Egypt, classical Greece, the Roman Empire, the British Empire, and the Inca Empire. Tell students that they are to research the civilization or empire, make a bulletin board display of what they learn, and develop a group oral presentation for the rest of the class in which they use some (or all) of the items in the bulletin board display. Assign each of

MORE

the groups one of the five bulletin board sections to use for its display.

3. Distribute The Rise and Fall of Peoples activity sheet. Go over the statements and questions with students. Tell them that this is some of the information they should include in their bulletin board displays and oral reports. Suggest that students also include information about art, architecture, clothing, economic systems, and forms of transportation.

*Day 2*

*Pre-class preparation:* Collect the art supplies students may need for their bulletin board displays.

1. As class begins, tell students what art supplies are available. Allow students to have the whole period to work on their projects. Remind students that everyone in their group should participate in the oral presentation and that such presentations usually go better if participants have rehearsed what they plan to say.
2. At the end of the period, tell students they should finish as homework any parts of their group's bulletin board display that haven't been completed.

*Day 3*

1. Have each group make its oral report to the rest of the class. Allow time after each presentation for other students to ask questions.
2. Go over each of the items on the activity sheet with students. Help the class come to see how each of the groups they have studied fits the patterns being described on the activity sheet.
3. Ask students to suggest other patterns that these groups followed, such as a level of technology, a general consensus on religious beliefs, and styles of clothing.
4. As a concluding activity, have students write in their journals. Ask students to think about the United States and write how it does or does not fit the patterns of the groups they studied. Tell students to refer to the activity sheet for ideas.

**Evaluation:**

Students should be able to list some patterns that civilizations and empires have often followed.

Students should be able to research and report on a specific civilization or empire and relate it to the pattern usually followed by other civilizations and empires.

NAME ______________________ CLASS ____________ DATE ____________

# THE RISE AND FALL OF PEOPLES

All civilizations and empires follow certain patterns. Read the statements and then answer the questions for the group you are studying. Write your answers on another sheet of paper as necessary.

**1.** Civilizations and empires of the past have a name by which they are usually known. What is the name of your group? ____________

**2.** Each civilization and empire had a specific time period during which it was most powerful. During what time period was your group most powerful? ____________

**3.** Civilizations and empires arise in specific geographic areas, even if they later expand their control. In what geographic area did your group arise? ____________

**4.** Most civilizations and empires have a single political system that they follow, even if this system changes somewhat over time. What was the political system used by your group? ____________

**5.** Most civilizations and empires include speakers of many different languages, but one language predominates. What was the major language used by your group? ____________

**6.** Powerful civilizations and empires usually have a few people who lead or greatly influence the group. Who were some of these people in your group? ____________

**7.** Powerful civilizations and empires often decline because citizens no longer accept that major beliefs are correct or are worth sacrificing for. What caused your group to decline? ____________

**8.** Great civilizations and empires usually leave behind houses, temples, castles, and other buildings that often are visited by tourists today. What modern-day country might tourists visit and what would they see of your group? ____________

**9.** Most powerful civilizations have influenced others. How did your group influence the United States? ____________

 

## 2.6 UNDERSTANDING WHY PEOPLE LIVE WHERE THEY DO

### GUIDING QUESTION 2: What are some subject area patterns?

**SUBJECT AREAS:** Language Arts, Social Studies

**GROUPING:** Whole class, individuals

**MATERIALS:** Wall map or overhead transparency of the world and, if necessary, an overhead projector;
Atlases showing precipitation and temperature;
Student group display of ancient Egypt (from lesson 2.5);
Laminated, desk-size world maps with relief, 1 per student;
Water-soluble pens, 1 per student

**BLOOM'S TAXONOMY LEVEL:** Knowledge, Comprehension, Inference, Analysis, Synthesis, Evaluation

**PRODUCTS AND OUTCOMES:** Marked desk maps;
lists of features of successful and unsuccessful patterns of human settlement

**TIME FRAME:** 1 class period

---

### Procedure:

*Pre-class preparation:* Be sure that the display of ancient Egypt from lesson 2.5 is still on the bulletin board or easily available to students. If necessary, set up the overhead projector.

1. Ask a volunteer to locate present-day Egypt on the wall map or overhead transparency. Ask two other volunteers to go to the bulletin board and study the student display on ancient Egypt to discover how the geography of ancient Egypt affected life there. (During this time, hand out the desk maps and water-soluble pens to the class for use in step 3 below.) Then ask the two volunteers to tell how geography affected the pattern of human settlement of ancient Egypt. The geographic factors include: farming patterns based on the Nile's yearly floods, use of the Nile as a major transportation route and source of fresh water, and buildings made from mud bricks since there were few trees.
2. Ask students to relate geographic factors of life in ancient Egypt to successful settlement elsewhere: the availability of arable land, a climate suitable for growing crops every year, steady supplies of fresh water, and the availability of other valuable resources (although exactly what resources are looked upon as valuable may change over time). Ask a

MORE

volunteer to write these factors on the board under the heading Geographic Factors Needed for Patterns of Successful Settlement. Then ask students to name factors that could make settlement difficult, such as very cold or hot climates, poor soil for farming, few natural resources, and little fresh water. Have a volunteer write suggested factors on the board. Use the heading Geographic Factors Causing Patterns of Unsuccessful Settlement.

3. Have students study their desk maps. Ask them to circle land areas where geographic factors probably allow for successful human settlement and put Xs on land areas where settlement would be difficult. Suggest that students refer to the atlases for help. Then ask volunteers to tell where they marked circles and Xs and why. Students should come to see that successful human settlement usually follows a pattern of temperate climates, good land for growing crops, and availability of other resources.
4. Discuss how most land areas have had some settlement, mostly as a result of human ingenuity, but that basic factors of geography have greatly influenced the size and longevity of the settlement. Use the Inuit or Eskimo of northern Canada and the Aborigines of Australia as examples of peoples who overcame geographical handicaps to live where they do. Ask students to name the geographic factors that hindered settlement growth for these peoples.
5. Talk about the changing value of some natural resources over time as a factor in the pattern of human settlement. Present the example of oil as a natural resource that was little used before the mid-1800s but is now one that greatly affects where people live. Help students come to see that human settlements have arisen in some areas, such as northern Alaska, because of oil resources there, while the use of oil to run automobiles has allowed for the growth of suburbs.
6. Tell students that in 1890, some 65 percent of Americans were farmers but by 1990, less than 5 percent of Americans were farmers. Ask students to name jobs people in urban areas often have, such as working in offices and stores. Point out that these jobs require many people to live near one another and that they have little relationship to geography. Ask students to name other things in the United States today that affect where people live, such as good transportation systems and an educated work force, as in the Silicon Valley area of California. Students should come to see that key influences affecting patterns of human settlement can change over time.

**Evaluation:**

Students should be able to name some key factors that have made up the general pattern of successful human settlement.

Students should be able to describe how patterns of settlement in the United States today are different from what they were in the past.

# 2.7 FINDING THE "STYLE" IN ART

## GUIDING QUESTION 2: What are some subject area patterns?

**SUBJECT AREAS:** Social Studies, the Arts

**GROUPING:** Individuals, whole class

**MATERIALS:** A large supply of art books with reproductions of paintings, sculpture, etc., by period;
Overhead projector and several blank transparencies;
Drawing paper, paints, brushes, scissors, glue, colored paper, and other art supplies

**BLOOM'S TAXONOMY LEVEL:** Knowledge, Comprehension, Analysis, Application, Synthesis

**PRODUCTS AND OUTCOMES:** Completed art pieces;
oral presentations;
bulletin board displays

**TIME FRAME:** 2 class periods

---

**Procedure:**

*Pre-class preparation:* Set up the overhead projector; collect the art history books. Copy examples of ancient Egyptian, Renaissance, Impressionist, and Modern periods of art onto overhead transparencies. Some good choices are:

- an Egyptian wall painting as an example of ancient art
- Jan van Eyck's *Arnolfini Marriage* or da Vinci's *Last Supper* as examples of Renaissance art
- Monet's *Water Lilies* or *St. Lazare Railroad Station* as examples of Impressionist art
- paintings from Andy Warhol's Marilyn Monroe series or his Campbell's Soup Can series as examples of Modern art

*Day 1*

1. Begin by telling students that just as there are patterns in math, science, history, and other subject areas, there are patterns in art. In these artistic patterns, artists, usually within the same historic period, follow a pattern in the art they create. These patterns include choice of subjects, medium, and colors. In this lesson, students will learn about some major patterns, or periods, in art history, create examples in those styles, and describe their works to the rest of the class.

MORE

2. Use the overhead transparencies to show students examples of the four periods they will be studying. Go through the overheads in historical order. Talk about each example in terms of what makes it representative of that period or style. For example, discuss perspective in the Egyptian wall painting and the blurred focus of Impressionist works. Be sure students understand that these examples are only some of the historical periods, or patterns, in the history of art.
3. Distribute the art history books. Tell students to look through the books, select a historical period to illustrate, and create an image in the style of that pattern or period on drawing paper. Encourage students, if they wish, to select periods or artistic patterns that were not among the examples you showed the class. Have students set aside some space at the bottom of their papers to write out how their illustrations follow the pattern of a specific period. Give students the rest of this class to work on the assignment.

*Day 2*

1. Give students some time at the beginning of class to finish their illustrations and write their accompanying descriptions.
2. Go around the class, having students present and discuss their illustrations, telling how their illustrations exemplify the period they chose. Allow students to discuss one another's images if they wish.
3. After all students have presented their illustrations, have students group themselves into artistic periods and attach their illustrations to the bulletin board in those groupings. Have one person from each group make a large label that names the artistic period. Hang the label on the bulletin board, above the illustrations it describes.
4. As a concluding activity, have students suggest ways that the artistic patterns or periods are similar to and different from one another. Create a T-chart on the board using the overall heading Artistic Patterns and the subheads of Similarities and Differences. Have volunteers use students' suggestions to fill in the chart.

**Evaluation:**

Students should be able to name some major periods of art history.

Students should be able to define a period of art history and create an illustration in that style.

Students should be able to name similarities and differences among various artistic periods.

## 2.8 HEALTHFUL EATING

### GUIDING QUESTION 2: What are some subject area patterns?

**SUBJECT AREAS:** Math, Science, Language Arts, Social Studies, Health/Physical Education

**GROUPING:** Whole class, individuals

**MATERIALS:** Food Pyramid activity sheet, 1 per student;
Two or three examples of packaged junk food with nutrition labeling;
Student journals

**BLOOM'S TAXONOMY LEVEL:** Knowledge, Comprehension, Analysis, Application, Synthesis

**PRODUCTS AND OUTCOMES:** Completed food lists for each of the food pyramid categories;
completed Food Pyramid Activity Sheets;
analyses of junk food contents;
journal entry

**TIME FRAME:** 1 class period

---

**Procedure:**

1. Start the period by telling students that this lesson will focus on issues of personal health and how students can make choices of food patterns that can affect their own health, both for good and for ill. Tell students they are going to begin by studying what they eat.
2. Distribute the Food Pyramid Activity Sheet. Tell students that these food guidelines were developed by the United States Departments of Agriculture and Health and Human Services. Go through each of the six categories in the food pyramid, asking students to name as many items in each category as they can. Have a volunteer write the items, by category, on the board as students name them.
3. Then ask students to complete the bottom portion of the Food Pyramid Activity Sheet. Remind students that each day's meals should include the recommended amounts of each category. Also tell students that no two days of meals should be the same.
4. Allow a reasonable amount of time for students to fill out the Food Pyramid Activity Sheet. Then ask each student to read one day's menu aloud to the rest of the class. After each student reads his or her menu, allow the rest of the class to make comments or ask questions as appropriate.

MORE

5. Talk with students about necessary vitamins, minerals, proteins, carbohydrates, and other nutrients that foods provide for good health. Help students come to see that eating the recommended foods will help them give their bodies the nutrients they need to be healthy.
6. Ask students to think about so-called junk foods, such as barbecued potato chips, candy bars, and ice cream. Hand out the junk food samples to student volunteers. Ask the volunteers to read the nutrition labels aloud to the rest of the class. As each label is read, help students come to realize the huge daily percentages of fat, cholesterol, and sodium that these items typically contain. Point out that these foods usually contain few if any vitamins and other necessary nutrients.

   Be sure students recognize that just a few of these junk food items can easily contain a whole day's recommended amount of items such as fat. This can be done by having students look at the daily percentages that the labels say the items contain. For example, point out that if a candy bar contains 40 percent of a day's recommended fat intake, that leaves just 20 percent for each of three meals, and that 20 percent for dinner would be consumed by a dinner-size serving of spaghetti with plain sauce, but would not allow for Parmesan cheese, garlic bread, or salad dressing.

   Talk about the portion sizes indicated on the nutrition labels of some junk foods. Help students see that eating just one so-called serving is sometimes not a realistic quantity and therefore the amount of fat and sodium, etc., being eaten may be much higher than what is indicated for a single serving when the food is actually consumed.
7. As a concluding activity, ask students to write in their journals. Have them describe how they might change their own eating habits to better meet the recommendations of the Food Pyramid.

**Evaluation:**

Students should be able to name the six categories of foods in the Food Pyramid and give examples of items in each.

Students should be able to create daily menus that comply with the recommendations of the Food Pyramid.

Students should be able to list some of the problems for healthful eating caused by so-called junk foods.

Students should be able to write down ways they might improve their own eating habits.

NAME ______________________ CLASS __________ DATE __________

# FOOD PYRAMID ACTIVITY SHEET

Study the food categories. Then create five days of healthful meals for yourself in the space provided.

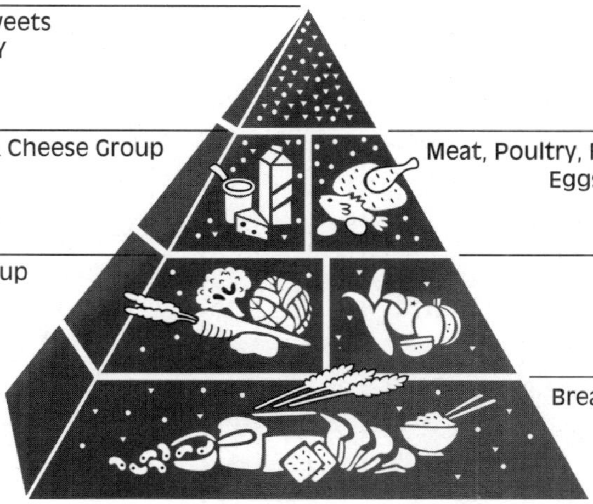


*Day 1*

Breakfast: ______________________

Lunch: ______________________

Dinner: ______________________

*Day 2*

Breakfast: ______________________

Lunch: ______________________

Dinner: ______________________

*Day 3*

Breakfast: ______________________

Lunch: ______________________

Dinner: ______________________

*Day 4*

Breakfast: ______________________

Lunch: ______________________

Dinner: ______________________

*Day 5*

Breakfast: ______________________

Lunch: ______________________

Dinner: ______________________

# MASTER ACTIVITY PLAN

## Guiding Question 3: How do people use patterns?

| Activities/Description | Math | Science | Language Arts | Social Studies | Health/Physical Ed. | The Arts | Time |
|---|---|---|---|---|---|---|---|
| **3.1** Playing the Election Game: How People Use the U.S. Pattern of Regular Elections–analyzing past elections and using that information to map out actions for various people and groups in a future election | ✔ | | ✔ | ✔ | | | 2 class periods |
| **3.2** Studying How People Use Patterns of Climate and Geography in Their Lives—analyzing how climate and geography affect the everyday lives of people and finding patterns in the effects in different regions | ✔ | ✔ | ✔ | ✔ | | ✔ | 3-4 class periods |

# 3.1 PLAYING THE ELECTION GAME: HOW PEOPLE USE THE U.S. PATTERN OF REGULAR ELECTIONS

## GUIDING QUESTION 3: How do people use patterns?

**SUBJECT AREAS:** Math, Language Arts, Social Studies

**GROUPING:** Whole class, small groups

**MATERIALS:** The Election Game activity sheet, 1 per student;
A long sheet of butcher paper;
Marking pens and colored paper in several different colors;
Thumb tacks;
Newsmagazines and articles

**BLOOM'S TAXONOMY LEVEL:** Knowledge, Comprehension, Inference, Analysis, Application, Synthesis, Evaluation

**PRODUCTS AND OUTCOMES:** Completed time lines

**TIME FRAME:** 2 class periods

**Note:** *Students may need to read newsmagazines and/or news articles to learn what might be the appropriate actions for their assigned roles. If necessary, assign roles according to whether good news articles can be found to describe them.*

---

**Procedure:**

*Pre-class preparation:* Collect newsmagazines and/or photocopy selected articles describing the most recent presidential campaign. Good magazine choices are *Time, Newsweek,* and *U.S. News and World Report.* One article for each of the roles you plan to assign should be sufficient.

*Day 1*

1. As an introduction, ask students to tell how often elections are held for senators (every six years); president (every four years); congressional representatives (every two years).
2. As background, point out to students that this election pattern has been going on for more than 200 years without interruption. This predictable pattern makes it possible for individuals and groups to make plans because they know what will happen when. Ask students to brainstorm a list of who some of these people and groups might be. Have a volunteer write the list on the board. The list might include:
   - people who want to run for office
   - the two major political parties, the Republicans and the Democrats

MORE

- people on the personal staffs of those now holding elective office
- groups such as political action committees (PACs) that want to give money to help elect candidates who favor the PAC's positions
- journalists who may be asked to cover stories about candidates
- TV network finance departments that will have to budget for election coverage, such as special election-night broadcasts
- people who might want to do volunteer work to help elect candidates with certain views
- companies that make political buttons, banners, and TV commercials

**3.** Divide the class into several small groups and distribute The Election Game activity sheets. Tell the groups that each will be assigned a role as a specific individual or group connected with the election. Have students read the activity sheet and assign the groups one of the following roles:

- a political party
- a political action committee
- a staff person for a candidate who is running for reelection
- an advertising agency working for one of the candidates
- a TV network
- a volunteer group with a specific political agenda

**4.** Pass out the newsmagazines and/or news articles to the groups. Point out that the groups can get help deciding what actions they should take by reviewing the news reports of how real people have acted in these situations. Student groups should decide what they will do at each time indicated on the activity sheet.

**5.** Allow students to spend the rest of the class working together in their small groups. As the period ends, remind students to bring their activity sheets to class tomorrow.

*Day 2*
*Pre-class Preparation*: Hang up the long piece of butcher paper horizontally on the bulletin board with thumb tacks and create a time line on the butcher paper. Divide the time line into the segments shown on the activity sheet.

**1.** Tell the class that today they are going to create a group time line on the bulletin board. The time line will show what each of the individuals or groups involved in the election would do at various stages in the election process. (At this point you may want to briefly discuss how time lines can be either vertical, as the activity sheet is, or horizontal, as the one on the bulletin board is, but still show the same relationships among items.)

MORE

2. Ask the groups to select the colors they want to use for the time line. (Avoid colors such as yellow that are very hard to distinguish when used for writing.) Each group should use a different color so that it will be easy to tell which items pertain to which person or group in the election process. Help students make a key at one end of the time line that explains the colors. Then have the groups write their plans on the time line.
3. After all the groups have completed their work, discuss the completed time line with students. Help students see that many different tasks are going on at the same time, depending on the group or individual involved. Talk about how knowledge of a regular pattern of elections allows people to make plans that are efficient and useful.

   Point out that some countries, such as Great Britain, France, and Italy use a political system that requires elections to be called a specific time from the last election, but also allows for elections to be held sooner under certain circumstances, such as a no-confidence vote in parliament. Ask students to suggest how this variable election date might affect choices, such as when candidates might begin asking supporters for financial contributions.
4. As a concluding activity, talk with students about countries with no regular elections or with elections that are just shams because only one candidate runs for each office. Some of these countries are Iraq, Cuba, and China. Help students come to see that not being able to count on having real choices can lead to violent upheavals, repressive governments, and as in the case of the Soviet Union, a collapse of the state, because citizens cannot vote for those who can be expected to reflect their views.

**Evaluation:**

Students should be able to recognize the pattern of regular elections in the United States.

Students should be able to name types of individuals and groups whose activities are influenced by the pattern of elections in the United States.

Students should be able to state how being able to express one's views at the ballot box helps create an orderly society.

NAME ______________________ CLASS __________ DATE __________

# THE ELECTION GAME

Our group is: ______________________________

12 Months before the Election

6 Months before the Election

2 Months before the Election

2 Weeks before the Election

2 Days before the Election

ELECTION DAY YOUR CANDIDATE WINS

1 Day after the Election

1 Week after the Election

2 Months after the Election

 • 

# 3.2 STUDYING HOW PEOPLE USE PATTERNS OF CLIMATE AND GEOGRAPHY IN THEIR LIVES

## GUIDING QUESTION 3: How do people use patterns?

**SUBJECT AREAS:** Math, Science, Language Arts, Social Studies, the Arts

**GROUPING:** Whole class, small groups, individuals

**MATERIALS:** Atlases, geographic encyclopedias, state tourist books and brochures, and other reference books;
A roll of butcher paper;
Several sets of colored drawing pens;
Thumb tacks;
Student journals

**BLOOM'S TAXONOMY LEVEL:** Knowledge, Comprehension, Inference, Analysis, Application, Synthesis, Evaluation

**PRODUCTS AND OUTCOMES:** Lists of activities by season and climate; group reports on various states; journal entry

**TIME FRAME:** 3-4 class periods

---

**Procedure:**

*Day 1*
*Pre-class preparation:* Collect the atlases and other reference books and set them aside in an easily accessible area of the classroom.

1. At the start of the period, ask students to name things that they do in various seasons of the year, such as using suntan lotion in the summer and wearing coats in the winter. Have a volunteer write the suggestions on the board under four headings: Spring, Summer, Fall, Winter.
2. After the class has created a fairly extensive list of seasonal activities, ask students to discuss what they know about differences in climate between regions in the United States, such as between Minnesota and southern California. Then have the class label items on the board according to a region's climate. For example, items suitable for Minnesota in the winter might be labeled M/W, while ones suitable for southern California in the fall might be labeled C/F. If necessary, point out that the same activity might be done in two or more seasons in the same climate or be done in different climates in different seasons. Help students come to see that differences in climate cause people to have different living patterns.

MORE

3. Now have students think about geography, again using Minnesota and southern California as examples. Suggest that Minnesota has the right climate for winter skiing, but the flat geography of the state makes downhill skiing much less common than cross-country skiing. At the same time, snow skiing is not an option in many parts of California, but the state's mountain ranges do create opportunities for downhill skiing in some seasons, quite close to areas that virtually never get even a trace of snow. Use this example as a starting point for discussing how climate and geography are intertwined in the creation of a pattern of human living.
4. Divide the class into six groups. Tell the groups that they are going to research and report on various states in the United States. Their reports will focus on the climate and geography of their assigned states and how those factors have led to the creation of patterns of living in the region. To get a good cross section of the types of climate and geography in the United States, some good states to assign to groups for research are Arizona, Florida, Iowa, Maine, Washington, and Wisconsin. You may wish to add your own state to this list of assignments or use it in place of one of those suggested.
5. Go through the types of reference books students will have available to use for their research, and tell students that they should cut off large sheets of the butcher paper to use as the background for their maps, lists, and descriptions, etc. Allow students to move their desks around so everyone in a group is sitting near one another.
6. Tell students that their group reports should include the following items (you may want to write this list on the board):
   - A **map** of the state that shows key physical aspects, including major rivers, lakes, mountain ranges, swamps, and deserts, as well as key political features such as cities, state boundaries, national parks or forests, and other effects of human settlement, such as theme parks and historic sites
   - A **graph** of average temperatures and precipitation for each month of the year (If there is a wide variation from region to region within the state, suggest that students graph the temperature and precipitation for the state capital.)
   - A **list** of major natural resources in the state and a **description** of how these resources are used by the people there
   - An **essay** that describes the state's major patterns of climate and geography and how people there use these patterns in their daily lives and work
7. Tell students that they have the rest of this class period and all of the next period to work on their group reports. Also tell students that their group reports should include everyone in a group in some way.

MORE

*Day 2*

1. Tell students that they have all of this period to work on their reports.
2. Point out to students that their displays should have an overall heading that prominently lists the state they are studying.
3. Encourage students to rehearse their oral presentations. As appropriate, give students help in making notes for their speeches, deciding who should speak about what and in which order, and ways they might use the maps and graphs in their speeches.

*Days 3 and 4*

1. Give the student groups a short time at the start of class to finish their reports. Then have each group present its report to the rest of the class. As each group finishes its report, have students hang the completed work on the bulletin board.
2. After all the groups have made their presentations, allow the whole class to get up and move around the room to study each group report in greater detail. After an appropriate amount of time, ask students to return to their desks.
3. Have a class discussion about how people in the United States use the patterns of climate and geography in their states in their daily lives. Some of the suggested patterns may be:
   - selecting vacation sites and times of year
   - choosing styles of housing and special features of those houses
   - deciding how to spend family resources on clothing
   - making choices from among the kinds of jobs available

   Ask a volunteer to write the suggestions on the board as others in the class name them. Have students name one or two examples of each pattern as it is listed on the board. Students should come to understand that knowledge about patterns of geography and climate can have a major influence on the individual decisions that people make about their own lives.
4. As a concluding activity, have students write in their journals about how they use knowledge of the climate and geography of your state in their own daily lives.

**Evaluation:**

Students should be able to name seasonal patterns of activities and tell which of these are influenced by a region's climate and geography.

Students should be able to work in a group to research and report on a specific state.

Students should be able to identify ways that people use knowledge about climate and geography to shape patterns of living.

Students should be able to describe how they use knowledge about your state's climate and geography in their own lives.

## FINAL ACTIVITY 1/CREATING T-SHIRT PATTERNS

**Subject Areas:** the Arts

**Grouping:** Small groups, whole class

**Materials:** Plain white T-shirts in appropriate sizes, 1 per student;
Waterproof, colored marking pens;
Beads, thread, scissors, and needles

**Bloom's Taxonomy Level:** Knowledge, Comprehension, Inference, Analysis, Application, Synthesis, Evaluation

**Products and Outcomes:** Completed T-shirts;
a list of statements that describe the T-shirt patterns

**Time Frame:** 2 class periods

---

**Procedure:**

*Pre-class preparation:* Purchase the T-shirts. Collect the art materials and set them aside in a convenient area of the room. In addition, the day before the lesson, you may want to warn students not to wear their best clothes the next day since they will probably be working with permanent markers.

*Day 1*

1. Tell students that as a final activity, they are going to work in groups to create patterns on T-shirts. Divide the class into several small groups. Give each student an appropriately sized T-shirt.
2. Tell students that each group should create a pattern that will be apparent when all the T-shirts from a group are shown together. Suggest that this means the patterns could either be visible or repeated on each T-shirt individually and/or among the shirts in a group; for example, each T-shirt has one word of a saying that can be read if the T-shirts are shown together in the correct order.
3. Tell students that they have all of this period and most of the next one to create and complete their T-shirts and that they will have to make a short group presentation about their T-shirt patterns when they are done. Show the materials students have available to create their patterns. Warn students to be careful using the permanent markers so as not to mar their clothes.

MORE

**4.** Suggest to students that their patterns need not be created in only one "medium." For example, colored markers and beads might be used together. Also point out that how students choose to display their T-shirts can become another pattern.

*Day 2*

*Pre-class preparation:* Be sure that sufficient supplies, such as thread and beads, are available for students to complete their projects. Provide additional supplies as necessary.

**1.** Begin the period by pointing out to students any additional supplies that may now be available for their projects.

**2.** About halfway through the period, point out to students how much time they have left to complete their projects.

**3.** Have each group make a short presentation of its T-shirts to the rest of the class. Allow others in the class to ask questions or discuss the patterns created by each group.

**4.** As a concluding activity, ask students to develop statements that can summarize or describe the patterns created by the class. Have a volunteer write the statements on the board as students suggest them. Help students come to see how the same basic idea can be creatively interpreted in a variety of equally successful but different ways.

**Evaluation:**

Students should be able to work in groups to develop patterns and then recreate them on T-shirts.

## FINAL ACTIVITY 2/CREATING A DANCE PATTERN

**Subject Areas:** Language Arts, Health/Physical Ed., the Arts

**Grouping:** Small groups

**Materials:** A video camera;
Blank videotapes, 1 per group;
Audiocassettes of country and western songs;
Tape players, 1 per group;
A VCR and monitor;
Examples of line dances from the Internet, TV, or videos

**Bloom's Taxonomy Level:** Knowledge, Comprehension, Inference, Analysis, Application, Synthesis, Evaluation

**Products and Outcomes:** Completed videotapes

**Time Frame:** 2 class periods

---

**Procedure:**

*Pre-class preparation:* Collect the video equipment. Rent videotapes, make tapes from TV programs such as ones on the TNN channel, or down load examples from the Internet.

*Day 1*

1. Tell students that as a final activity, they are going to work in groups to create line dances and then make videotapes that can teach others their new dances. Play some of the samples for the class so that students gain an understanding of the line dance. Divide the class into several groups and give each group an audiotape player. Have the groups play the audiocassettes and select tunes they want to use.
2. Allow students to group themselves in different areas of the classroom to play their audiocassettes and work out the steps of their dances. Suggest that once the basic dance is created, the students in each group divide themselves into three subgroups of videographers, teachers, and demonstrators for the filming of their videotapes.

*Day 2*

1. Have students create their videotapes as they are ready to do so.
2. Show the completed videotapes to the whole class. Have volunteers from other groups perform each line dance after viewing a tape.

**Evaluation:**
Students should be able to work in groups to create teaching tools for demonstrating patterns to others.

NAME ______________________ CLASS __________ DATE __________

# EVALUATING MY GROUP'S FINAL ACTIVITY

Rate your group's final activity by commenting on the items listed below.

*Use of Various Materials and Resources to Complete the Project*

Things That Worked Well

______________________________

______________________________

______________________________

Things That Needed Improvement

______________________________

______________________________

______________________________

*Presentation of Information*

Things That Worked Well

______________________________

______________________________

______________________________

Things That Needed Improvement

______________________________

______________________________

______________________________

NAME ______________________________ CLASS __________ DATE __________

# EVALUATING HOW MY GROUP WORKED

*Evaluating My Performance in the Group*

Check the box that best describes how well you carried out each item below when working with your group.

| Performance area | Exemplary | Accomplished | Developing | Emerging |
|---|---|---|---|---|
| I played an active part in the group. | | | | |
| I cooperated with other members. | | | | |
| I suggested ideas to the group. | | | | |
| I completed my tasks on time. | | | | |
| I helped others in the group. | | | | |
| I did the best work that I could. | | | | |

*Evaluating How the Group Worked Together*

Write brief comments about how your group worked together.

| | What Worked Well | What Needed Improvement |
|---|---|---|
| How the group was organized | | |
| How the group cooperated | | |

 